TURN TO PAGE 23 FOR
HOW TO MAKE YOUR
Door Hanger.

SHHHHHHHH...

I feel cheerful

I feel cheerful

I feel cheerful

I feel cheerful

TURN TO PAGE 23 FOR
HOW TO MAKE YOUR
Door Hanger.

I'M SO RAZZMATAZZ
RIGHT NOW

I feel cheerful
I feel cheerful
I feel cheerful
I feel cheerful
I feel cheerful

TURN TO PAGE 22 FOR HOW TO MAKE YOUR MOOD CUBE.

Glue Here

Bold and Bluetiful!

© 2020 Crayola

Relaxed and Sunset Orange

Glue Here

Glue Here

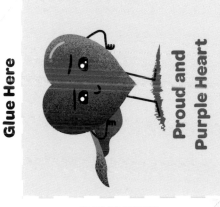

Glue Here

Proud and Purple Heart

əɹəH ənlꭹ

Happy and Mountain Meadow Green

Wild and Unmellow Yellow

Glue Here

əɹəH ənlꭹ

ʞuᴉd ǝW ǝlʞɔᴉⱢ puɐ ʎllᴉS

I feel cheerful

I feel cheerful

I feel cheerful

I feel cheerful

I feel cheerful

COZY

CONFIDENT

WILD

BOLD

CALM

PROUD

SILLY

WISE

RELAXED

HAPPY

COZY

CONFIDENT

RELAXED

WISE

CALM

PROUD

SILLY

HAPPY

BOLD

WILD

RAZZ MA TAZZ -TIC!

YOU TICKLE ME PINK!

I feel cheerful

I feel cheerful

I feel cheerful

I feel cheerful

I feel cheerful

IS MY COMFORT MOOD

THERE'S NO STOPPING
Unmellow
Yellow

I feel cheerful

A Granny Smith Apple A Day

PEACE, LOVE AND MOUNTAIN MEADOW

YOU LOOK *Bluetiful*

PURPLE HEART **PROUD**
PURPLE HEART **BRAVE**

I feel cheerful

I feel cheerful

I feel cheerful

I feel cheerful